National Parks: **The Lake District**

First published in 2018 by:
Northern Eye Books Limited

Northern Eye Books, Tattenhall, Cheshire CH3 9PX

Second edition published 2021
Third edition published in 2025

© Northern Eye Books Limited 2025

ISBN 978-1-908632-75-3

Text: *Vivienne Crow, Steve Goodier, Carl Rogers, Stewart Smith*

Series editor: *Carl Rogers*

Photographs: *Carl Rogers, Shutterstock, Dreamstime, Stewart Smith Photography*

Design: *Carl Rogers and Laura Hodgkinson*

A CIP catalogue record for this book is available from the British Library.

Printed in the UK on woodland-friendly FSC stock

Cover: *Sunlit Scots pines, Buttermere*

www.northerneyebooks.co.uk

@northerneyebooks
@carlrogers1960

@northerneyeboo

@northerneyebooks
@carlrogers1960

For sales enquiries, please call 01928 723 744

tony@northerneyebooks.co.uk

Important Advice: The routes described in this book are undertaken at the reader's own risk. Walkers should take into account their level of fitness, wear suitable footwear and clothing, and carry food and water. It is also advisable to take the relevant OS map with you in case you get lost and leave the area covered by our maps.

Whilst every care has been taken to ensure the accuracy of the route directions, the publishers cannot accept responsibility for errors or omissions, or for changes in the details given. Nor can the publisher and copyright owners accept responsibility for any consequences arising from the use of this book.

If you find any inaccuracies in either the text or maps, please write or email us at the address above. Thank you.

This book contains mapping data licensed from the Ordnance Survey with the permission of the Controller of Her Majesty's Stationery Office. © Crown copyright 2025 All rights reserved. Licence number AC0000833184

Contents

England's Largest National Park 4
Top 10 Walks: Best of the Best 6
1 | **Kirkstile Inn** 8
2 | **Aira Force** 12
3 | **Wastwater** 18
4 | **Tarn Hows** 24
5 | Around **Derwent Water** 30
6 | Around **Loweswater** 36
7 | **Castlerigg stone circle** 40
8 | **Catbells** 46
9 | **Scafell Pike** 52
10 | **Striding & Swirral Edges** 58
Useful Information 64

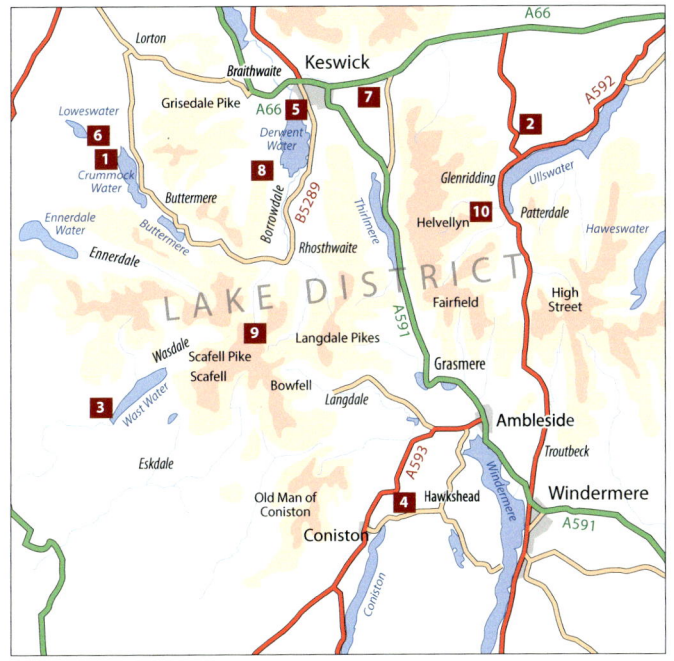

England's Largest National Park

THE LAKE DISTRICT NATIONAL PARK is the largest and most popular of the thirteen National Parks in England and Wales. Created as one of Britain's first National Parks in 1951, its role is to 'conserve and enhance' the natural beauty, wildlife and culture of this iconic English landscape, not just for residents and visitors today but for future generations, too.

Remarkably, the National Park contains every scrap of England's land over 3,000 feet, including its highest mountain, Scafell Pike. Packed within the Park's 912 square miles are numerous peaks and fells, over 400 lakes and tarns, around 50 dales, six National Nature Reserves, and more than 100 Sites of Special Scientific Interest—all publicly accessible on over 1,800 miles of footpaths and other rights of way. It's no surprise then, that the Lake District attracts an estimated 15 million visitors a year.

Buttermere's iconic Scots pines reflected in the lake

The very best of the Lake District

Part of the Lake District's unique attraction is its compactness. Within its boundaries are a rich mix of lakes, mountains, forests and farmland characterised by pretty villages, winding roads, deep dales and valleys, drystone walls and distinctive Herdwick and Swaledale sheep.

Ready to explore? Discover the two loveliest lakeside walks, the best pub walk, and the most amazing view. Visit Cumbria's stunning Castlerigg stone circle, scale its best-loved low and high fells, or marvel at its most dramatic waterfall. Every one is a walk to remember.

> "Oh, how can I put into words the joys of a walk over country such as this; the scenes that delight the eyes, the blessed peace of mind, the sheer exuberance which fills your soul?"
>
> Alfred Wainwright

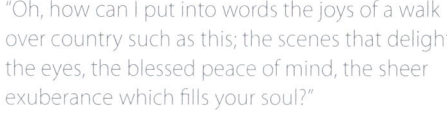

TOP 10 Walks: Lakeland's best themed walks

HERE, PACKED INTO A SINGLE POCKET-SIZE BOOK, are the ten absolute best short circular walks in the Lake District National Park. They've been carefully selected—from the already hugely-popular themed *Top 10 Walks: Lake District* series—to showcase the finest and most enjoyable walks across the Lakes. So, whether you fancy a stroll around a lake or tarn, a stunning view or a swift pint, or something more challenging, there's plenty to go at here. The choice is yours.

PUB WALK — Kirkstile Inn, Loweswater — page 8

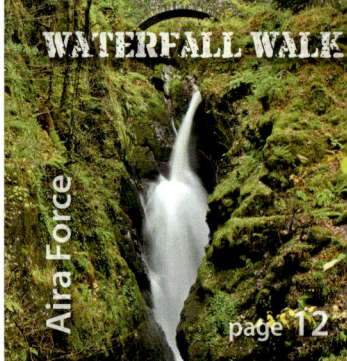

WATERFALL WALK — Aira Force — page 12

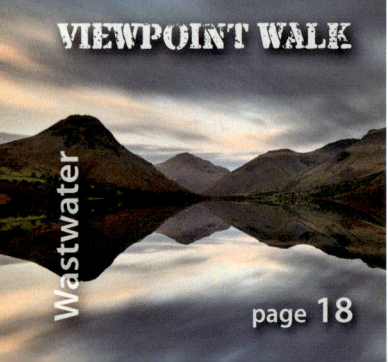

VIEWPOINT WALK — Wastwater — page 18

TARN WALK — Tarn Hows — page 24

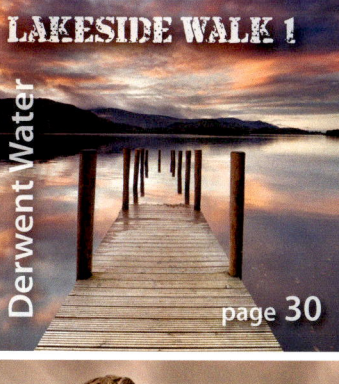
LAKESIDE WALK 1 — Derwent Water — page 30

LAKESIDE WALK 2 — Loweswater — page 36

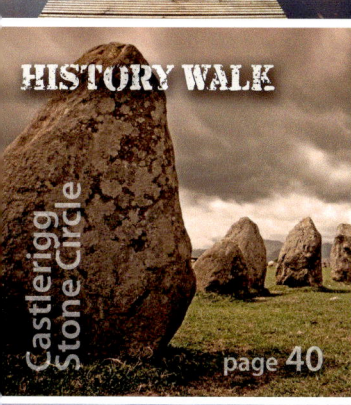
HISTORY WALK — Castlerigg Stone Circle — page 40

LOW FELL WALK — Catbells — page 46

HIGH FELL WALK — Scafell Pike — page 52

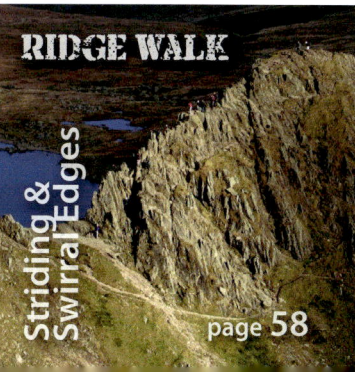
RIDGE WALK — Striding & Swirral Edges — page 58

Looking across Crummock Water to Grasmoor

PUB WALK

Kirkstile Inn
Loweswater

walk 1

What to expect: *Woodland and lakeside paths; good tracks; some road walking*

Distance/time: 8.5 kilometres / 5¼ miles. Allow 2½-3 hours
Start: Parking area next to Lanthwaite Green Farm near the northern end of Crummock Water, about 4.5 kilometres north of Buttermere
Grid ref: NY 159 208
Ordnance Survey Map: OL 4 The English Lakes North-western area. *Keswick, Cockermouth & Wigton*
The Pub: Kirkstile Inn, Loweswater, Cumbria CA13 0RU | 01900 85219 | www.kirkstile.com | info@kirkstile.com

Walk outline: This lovely walk links woodlands close to Crummock Water and the tiny village of Loweswater. It takes in everything from gnarled oaks to conifer stands, where there's a real chance of spotting rare red squirrels. Dropping to the lakeshore, the walk gives outstanding views of the fells surrounding this magnificent lake.

Tucked away between Loweswater and Crummock Water, the Kirkstile Inn is a classic Lakeland pub that has been providing food and shelter since Tudor times. Modern visitors can expect a relaxed atmosphere, low beams, open fires, good food and beer. There are two bars and a comfortable dining room.

Kirkstile Inn

▶ Kirkstile Inn at a glance
Open: Mon-Sat 11am-11pm; Sun 12 noon-10.30pm
Brewery/company: Free house with own brewery
Real ales: Loweswater Gold, Melbreak bitter, Coniston Bluebird, Grasmoor Dark, Yates bitter, guest beers
Food: Daily 12-2pm, 6-9pm. Excellent, rustic dishes with a Cumbrian focus. Specials board. Often busy, booking advisable
Rooms: Four rooms en-suite, plus family annexe
Outside: Lovely beer garden with 20 tables and a play area
Children & dogs: Children welcome. Dogs allowed in bar only

More pub walks......

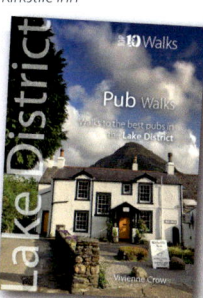

The Walk

1. From the parking area, turn left along the road. Just after the farm, cross the stile on your left. After the path swings right and just before it enters a field, go through the kissing-gate on your left and walk alongside the wall on the right.

2. After entering **Lanthwaite Woods**, follow the track and keep straight ahead at any junctions until you reach the gate leading into the car park. Go through this and continue to the road.

3. Turn left and walk along the asphalt for 700 metres, ignoring the first road junction as you pass the Loweswater sign. Then turn left along the lane signposted to the **Kirkstile Inn**.

4. With the pub directly in front of you, turn left and immediately right. Follow this lane to a gate in front of a stand of conifers. Go through and take the left fork. As you emerge from the trees, turn left to walk with the fence on your left. The path generally stays close to the fence/wall on the left, but it does briefly swing away from it as it descends.

5. Don't go through the gate in the wall corner near **Highpark**; instead, turn right along a faint, grassy path parallel with the wall on the left. As you look down on **Crummock Water**, bear left—staying with the wall—to descend to the lakeshore. At the water's edge, turn left through the gate. Keep to the lakeshore path, around the side of the **pumphouse** and across some bridges.

6. Soon after the final bridge, you reach a junction of paths near some benches. Take the narrow path on the right. This

A misty autumn sunrise at Crummock Water

joins a track from the left, which ends at a **boathouse**. A narrow path continues along the lakeshore. After leaving the woods, keep straight ahead. The trail becomes indistinct as it approaches the tumbledown end of a wall, but maintain the same line. After the wall, bear left to climb to the higher of two gates ahead. Beyond this, continue gently uphill. Bear left at a fork to reach a gate beside the road.

7. Turn left and walk along the asphalt for around one kilometre to return to the parking area. ♦

'Deep and solemn'

In his Guide to the Lakes, *the Romantic poet William Wordsworth was struck by the beauty of Crummock Water.* "... There is scarcely anything finer than the view from a boat in the centre of Crummock Water," he wrote. "The scene is deep, and solemn and lonely; and in no other spot is the majesty of the mountains so irresistibly felt as an omnipresence, or so passively submitted to as a spirit incumbent upon the imagination."

Aira Force, above Ullswater

WATERFALL WALK

Aira Force

Through an arboretum to spectacular waterfalls and on to a low fell with breathtaking views

walk 2

What to expect:
Clear paths, rough in places; low-lying fell

Distance/time: 6.5 kilometres/ 4 miles. Allow 2½-3 hours

Start: National Trust pay and display car park at Aira Force on A592, 2½ miles north-east of Glenridding

Grid ref: NY 400 200

Ordnance Survey Map: OL 5 *The English Lakes North-eastern area. Penrith, Patterdale & Caldbeck*

After the walk: Small café next to car park or choice of pubs and cafés in nearby Glenridding

Walk outline
Good paths lead through a wide and often exotic variety of trees to spectacular Aira Force. The route becomes a little rougher as it continues upstream, past High Force. Turning off on to what is, at first, a less well defined path, it then climbs at a moderate angle on to Gowbarrow Fell to complete a circuit of the top of the fell.

Aira Force and High Force
As Aira Beck flows from the northernmost hills of the Helvellyn range, it gradually gathers volume and momentum on its journey to Ullswater. The first of the falls it forms as it enters the Aira gorge is High Force, a series of dramatic cascades. Losing height at an ever increasing rate, it then thunders downstream in a whirling torrent until, finally, it reaches its crescendo and plummets a massive twenty-one metres to form Aira Force, one of the most stunning waterfalls in the Lake District. At the foot of this tremendous drop are sheer-sided pools, and, all around, trees cling to the edges of the ravine. It's a magnificent, even daunting sight.

Gowbarrow Fell summit

More walks to waterfalls ....

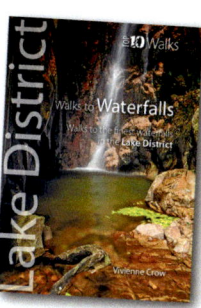

The Walk

1. Walk to the far end of the car park to join the popular path heading up towards **Aira Force**. Keep right at a fork and you'll soon reach an area of **ancient yews and towering conifers**.

Turn left here, away from the iron railings on the right, to slowly ascend, with the beck on your right, to a bench. Turn right to descend the steep stone staircase to the base of powerful **Aira Force**, feeling the spray from the falls on your face.

The drama of this setting has inspired many writers, and the poet William Wordsworth, who was a frequent visitor to the area, wrote no fewer than three poems about Aira Force. The most well known of these is The Somnambulist. *This tells the local legend of two lovers who were parted by war. As the knight went off to fight, his sweetheart was left at home, worrying about him. Her anxiety led her to start sleepwalking along the edge of the steep Aira gorge. When the knight returned, he discovered her asleep and in this precarious position. He touched her and she awoke, lost her balance and fell to her death.*

2. Cross the bridge at the bottom of the falls and turn left

© Crown copyright and/or database right. All rights reserved. Licence number AC0000833184

The northern end of Ullswater from the summit of Gowbarrow Fell

immediately—up another steep, stone stairway, to join a path coming in from the right. Here, a brief detour to the left takes walkers on to the stone **humpback bridge** at the top of the noisy falls.

Back on the main path, there is quite a bit of clambering to be done as you wend your way upstream. In a couple of hundred metres, you will see a path branching left to a wooden footbridge below. Ignore this, and continue, with the beck on your left, past **High Force.** The trees thin out after you pass through a gap in a wall and then disappear entirely beyond a gate.

3. Just before another gate—a small, wooden gate beside a larger farm gate—turn right to start climbing on a faint path. Go through the gate and head steeply uphill with the wall on your left. After 700 metres of uphill slog, the path finally levels off slightly and swings right—away from the wall—towards the Ordnance Survey 'trig' point on the summit of **Gowbarrow Fell**.

4. Descend north-east at first, then follow the clear path round to the bracken-

Gowbarrow Fell enjoys superb views across Ullswater to Place Fell and Helvellyn

smothered remains of an **old shooting hut** on the eastern edge of the fell.

5. Bear right here. Around one kilometre beyond the ruin, you round the side of a crag and are suddenly met by arguably the most **magnificent panorama** in the eastern Lakes.

Breathtaking is an over-used adjective, but, on this occasion, it is hard to resist that sharp intake of breath as the western expanse of Ullswater is revealed with the dark, craggy Helvellyn range in the background. This is a place to linger—and, conveniently, there is a bench nearby.

With that amazing view of Ullswater directly ahead, the path descends.

*As you lose height, you will see what looks like a medieval tower below. This is **Lyulph's Tower** and isn't as old as it looks; it was built as a shooting lodge in 1780.*

6. You eventually reach a junction of paths close to the edge of the fenced woodland at **Aira Gorge**. Bear left to go through a small gate. A couple of paths join from the right as you descend through the trees. Cross a bridge over **Aira Beck** and then keep straight ahead—up the steps and with iron railings on your left. After a gate, follow the clear path, keeping left when it forks, to return to the car park.

Many of the trees in the arboretum around

Aira Force were planted by the Howard family of Greystoke. They were lords of the manor here from the late Middle Ages until they sold the land to the National Trust in 1906. The fine specimens include a Douglas fir that is said to be the tallest tree in Cumbria, some ancient yews and a Chilean pine or 'Monkey Puzzle' tree. There are also two huge sitka spruces, dating back to 1846. The largest has a girth of more than six metres. ♦

Wild daffodils

The woods below Gowbarrow are said to have inspired Wordsworth to write his most famous poem, Daffodils. Having walked there with him in April 1802, his sister Dorothy noted in her diary: "I never saw daffodils so beautiful..." Two years later, he used her subsequent observations as the basis of a poem, the first line of which is probably the most famous in English poetry: "I wandered lonely as a cloud..."

Sunset tints the view up Wastwater to Yewbarrow and Lingmell

WALK TO A VIEWPOINT

walk 3

Wastwater

A low level walk around the lakeshore with tremendous views up the lake to the mountains

What to expect:
Farm tracks, open fields, woodland and lakeshore paths

Distance/time: 8 kilometres/ 5 miles. Allow 2½ - 3 hours

Start: Small car park at Cinderdale Bridge, Nether Wasdale

Grid ref: NY 128 038

Ordnance Survey Map: Explorer OL6 The English Lakes Southwestern area. *Coniston, Ulverston and Barrow in Furness*

After the walk: The Strands Inn, Nether Wasdale CA20 1ET | www.thestrandsinn.com | 01946 726237

Walk outline

A farm track leads away from the road to take you on an idyllic route through fields and then woodland, with hints of the rugged mountain views to follow. Heading beneath Wasdale screes beside the River Irt, you then follow the southern and western shores of Wastwater accompanied by the classic views up the length of the lake towards Yewbarrow, Great Gable, Lingmell and the Scafell massif, before returning via Greendale.

Wastwater

One of England's most famous mountain views, and the one that forms the logo of the National Park authority, is most often reached by car and simply pulling off the road. Such views are, of course, more naturally and satisfyingly appreciated with a gentle reveal by foot.

This route begins by offering you views of the upper reaches of the higher summits as a teaser, before eventually revealing the full length of the mountains top down, with Wastwater itself being the final addition to the classic view

Approaching Wastwater

More walks to viewpoints ...

The Walk

1. Leave the car park at **Cinderdale bridge** via the entrance and turn right on to the road, crossing over the bridge. Around the corner two footpath signs to the left appear in quick succession. Take the first of these, heading down the farm track with Whin Rigg and the Wasdale screes catching all the attention up ahead. *As you crest a small hill and round the corner, a gate to the left invites you to linger over a taster of the higher mountain views to come.*

Continue on the track through **Easthwaite Farm** buildings and then through the gate where the tops of Yewbarrow and Great Gable lead you on ahead.

2. After 150 metres on your left you'll pass a gate next to a wall, which is marked private. Ignore this but immediately afterwards leave the track through another gate to the left on the other side of the wall. Continue through this field beside a wall then a hedge, then shortly before reaching the corner of the field bear left through a gate and into the next.

Follow the traces of a path towards **Lund Bridge**, which takes you across

© Crown copyright and/or database right. All rights reserved. Licence number AC0000833184

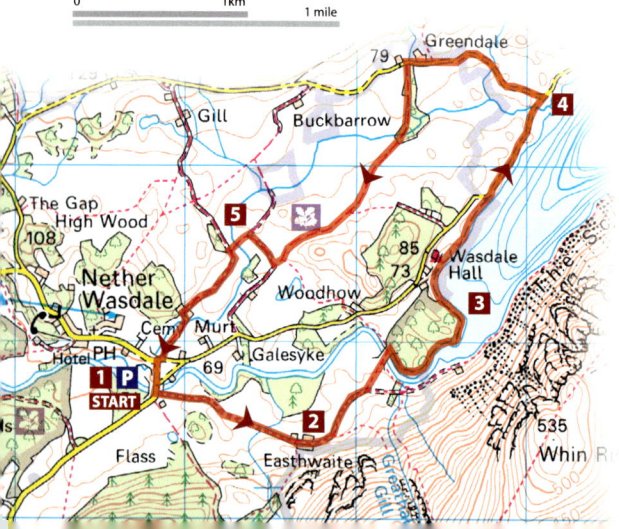

Whin Rigg and the Wastwater Screes on a perfect evening

the nascent **River Irt**. After crossing this stone bridge, bear immediately right through a gate and into **Low Wood**. The path forks instantly, where the right hand choice should be taken to follow the curve of the Irt for a while, until it widens to form an **enclosed pool** beside a picturesque **boathouse** at the southern end of **Wastwater**.

Pass beyond this on the path to soon reach the southern shore of the lake and your first wide open views of the mountains, with the imposing screes and the tricky base path off to the right.

3. Head along the southern shore along the well-maintained stony path, before passing through a gate and past the front lawn of the enviously situated 19th century **Wasdale Hall**, now one of the more grandiose Youth Hostels in the Lake District.

Continue through another gate to follow the path beneath trees, and through yet another along the now grassy **lake shore path**, before climbing the wall via a stile and bearing right onto the road. Carry on until you cross over the bridge and reach a junction, where you need

Yewbarrow, Great Gable and Lingmell seen across Wastwater

to reluctantly turn your back on the spectacular surroundings of Wastwater to turn left onto the **Gosforth road**.

4. There is some consolation as you are now confronted by the fine craggy lower fells of Buckbarrow and Middle Fell up ahead, which would form a more dominant presence over the landscape in most other situations.

For those with a surfeit of energy, the summit of the latter provides particularly fine views of the surrounding mountains.

For now, however, continue along the road passing through the tiny hamlet of **Greendale**, then head over the **bridge** and turn immediately left through a gate onto a bridleway. Carry on through the woods beside a field, crossing a **small bridge** as the path curves to the right, then over a stile and into the field. Follow the track ahead through another gate into the next field, then along the path and over the next stile onto a fenced in grassy track. Ignore a path which leaves to the left and then soon after turn right off the track on a bridleway signed for 'Buckbarrow'. Pass through another gate between two walls before reaching a junction beneath a line of trees.

5. Turn left here, then head though a gate into the field. Aim for another gate dead ahead, and once through this follow the wall to your left. Keep to this track passing beside **Mill Place** and eventually back onto the road close to your starting point. Turn right then immediately left, signposted for 'Santon Bridge and Drigg', which shortly brings you back to **Cinderdale bridge car park** to complete the walk. ♦

Britain's favourite view?

The vista along the length of England's deepest lake to the mountains surrounding Wasdale Head has been known unofficially as Britain's favourite view since winning a public vote on television several years ago. The view remains a true Lake District icon, and for those unable to climb to the summits of the higher fells, English mountain views don't get much more rugged and imperious than this.

Tarn Hows at dawn

WALK TO A TARN

Tarn Hows

A gentle saunter through undulating woods to one of Lakeland's most popular beauty spots

walk 4

What to expect:
Field and woodland paths, some tracks

Distance/time: 9.5 kilometres/6 miles. Allow 2½-3 hours

Start: Pay and Display car park beside the Tourist Information Centre in the centre of Coniston

Grid ref: SD 303 975

Ordnance Survey Map: OL 7 *The English Lakes South-eastern area Windermere, Kendal and Silverdale*

After the walk: Pubs, cafés and tearooms in Coniston

Walk outline
Starting from Coniston, this straightforward walk follows a series of paths across fields and through woods to the beautifully situated Tarn Hows. A constructed track does a circuit of this delightful body of water, after which the route descends beside the pretty cascades of Tom Gill. A series of farm paths, woodland trails and quiet lanes then returns the walker to Coniston.

Tarn Hows
Despite being man-made, Tarn Hows is well worth a visit. There used to be three tiny tarns here, but the single body of water you see today was created when the 19th-century industrialist James Marshall dammed one of them. With plans based on ideas of the 'picturesque' that were popular at the time, he wanted to create something beautiful. In so doing, he also planted the conifers surrounding the tarn, a feature that is intended both to frame and dramatically reveal views of his creation.

'Tramper' wheelchair

More walks to tarns ...

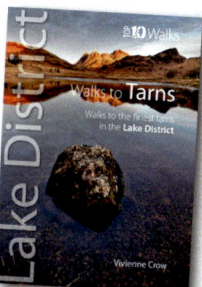

Contemplating Tarn Hows in the early morning before the crowds arrive

The Walk

1. From the **car park entrance** go ahead across '**Ruskin Avenue**' and turn right along the road (Tilberthwaite Avenue).

Follow the road to the edge of **Coniston** and immediately before a bridge, turn left into '**Shepherds Bridge Lane**'.

Follow the lane with the beck to your right and, opposite the primary school, take the signed footpath over the bridge on the right. Immediately after the bridge turn left along the bank to enter fields.

The path heads off across the field passing beneath a line of oaks and towards a **stone-built folly**.

This Gothic construction is probably the grandest and most fanciful kennel you will ever see. It was built by James Marshall, who was also responsible for the creation of Tarn Hows, after he became master of the Coniston foxhounds in 1839.

The path continues beside the folly on a gentle rise towards woods. Enter the woods by a kissing gate surrounded by **ancient yew trees** and walk ahead through the trees to enter fields again.

Follow the obvious path ahead through a large field and at the far end bear left to go through a gate. The path cuts directly through the next field aiming for a kissing gate in the far fence. This leads onto a **farm track**. Turn left along the track.

2. Follow the track to the old stone bridge but don't cross the bridge, instead, go through the small foot gate into the field directly ahead (signed to 'Tarn Hows'). Walk across the field to enter woods again by a kissing gate adjacent to **Yewdale Beck**. The path keeps beside the beck briefly, before veering right-wards to begin a gentle climb through the trees.

At the upper edge of the woods the path runs beside a wall and there are good views left across the valley into Yewdale.

Go through two gates ahead to reach the access road to a small cottage on the left. Turn right and follow the access road to a tarmac lane.

3. Turn left and walk up the lane to **Tarn Hows**.

Hidden from view until the last moment, Tarn Hows sits in a hollow surrounded by woods and low-lying fells. To the west, Wetherlam and the Coniston fells provide a craggy backdrop to the delightful scene.

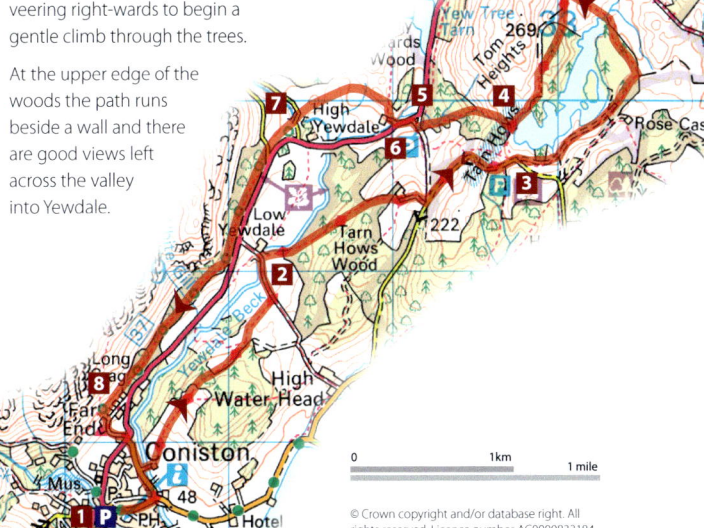

© Crown copyright and/or database right. All rights reserved. Licence number AC0000833184

A view across Tarn Hows to Wetherlam and the Coniston Fells

As the lane swing right, bear left onto a footpath which leads around the tarn in an anti-clockwise direction.

4. Immediately before the path crosses the outflow, take the signed footpath on the right ('Glen Mary, Yew Tree Tarn'). This hugs the rocky side of the beck which steepens into a series of picturesque cascades. The climax is **Tom Gill Waterfall,** a modest affair by Lakeland standards, set amid oak woods.

5. As you approach the road turn left over a footbridge and walk left through a small car park. At the end of the car park a permissive path enters fields to run parallel to the road. Almost opposite **Yew Tree Farm** on the right, go through the kissing gate on the right, cross the road and bear right to the farm access road.

6. Take the signed permissive bridleway to the right of the farm. At a fork ignore a path on the right continuing ahead on the well-made gravel surface.

7. At a narrow lane turn left over the little stone bridge, then bear right immediately on the bridleway which continues parallel to the road. Cross the Tilberthwaite lane and continue through woods below **Yewdale Fells** (2km).

8. Leave the woods by a small gate in the wall ahead and in 150 metres go left through a second gate. Walk down to the lane and turn right. At the next junction turn left, then immediately right into **Shepherds Bridge Lane**. Retrace the outward route to complete the walk. ♦

Monk Coniston estate

Tarn Hows is part of the Monk Coniston estate bought by James Marshall in 1835. In 1926, the hall and gardens were sold to John Bradshaw. Beatrix Potter bought the rest of the estate, including Tarn Hows, in 1930. She then sold half at cost price to the National Trust; the other half passed to the charity after her death in 1943. The National Trust reunited the estate in 1945 by purchasing the hall and gardens.

On the jetty at Hawes End, Derwent Water

LAKESIDE WALK

Around **Derwent Water**

A long but straightforward circuit of one of Lakeland's most beautiful and spectacular lakes

walk 5

What to expect:
Good lakeside and forest footpaths, one short road section. No ascents or descents

Distance/time: 11.75 kilometres/ 7½ miles. Allow 3-4 hours
Start: Large Pay and Display car park adjacent to the Theatre by the Lake, Keswick. Or car parks in Keswick and follow signs to the Theatre by the Lake
Grid ref: NY 265 229
Ordnance Survey Map: OL 4 *The English Lakes North-western area. Keswick, Cockermouth & Wigton*
After the walk: Pubs, cafés and restaurants in Keswick

Walk outline
Beginning with a boat trip across to Nichol End, good paths lead along the western shore, through the wooded parkland of Brandelhow and Manesty. At the head of the lake, a footbridge crosses the River Derwent followed by a short road section. The beautiful bays around Friar's Crag make a fine end to the circuit. The Derwent launches run daily and can be used to shorten the walk from any of the five stages around the lake.

Derwent Water
Ringed by magnificent fells and shoreside woods, Derwent Water is sometimes dubbed the 'Queen of the Lakes'. The third largest of the Cumbrian lakes, it stretches for three miles between the lakehead market town of Keswick in the north and beautiful Borrowdale in the south.

Regular motor launches leave from Keswick all year round, dropping off and picking up passengers at jetties around the lake. Combining an inexpensive boat trip with a leisurely walk along the tree-lined shore makes for a lovely half day, especially when combined with a lakeside picnic, paddle or swim in warm weather.

Boats for hire

More lakeside walks ...

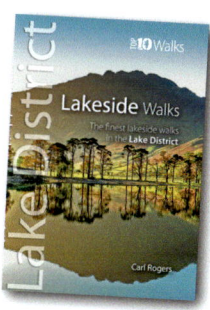

Brandelhow Park's stunted pines frame a view of distant Blencathra

The Walk

1. Turn left out of the car park and walk down to the landing stages. Take a launch across the lake to **Nichol End**.

2. From the **Nichol End** jetty, walk up the access road past the shop and café. Turn left along the drive immediately behind the café. Bear right off the drive, opposite a house on the left, and walk along a wide forestry track.

At a T-junction, turn left along the driveway to '**Lingholm**' and take the signed footpath to the right of the gateway (signed to 'Catbells'). Follow the path ahead through the woods.

Leave the woods by a gate and walk across a field, with **Catbells** rising ahead. Cross a footbridge and take the rising footpath ahead into the woods again.

At the end of the path, a gate leads onto an access road. Turn left along the road (ignore the first left) and in about 50 metres, bear left, off the road, onto a path signed to '**Hawes End Jetty**', which leads down to the lake shore.

3. Follow the path to the right along the shore. After a stile, the path moves

Walk 6 – Around **Derwent Water** ♦ 33

away from the shore to join a well-made gravel footpath. Head left, along the path, which soon swings left back towards the lake. Immediately after a gate, turn sharp left onto a path that leads back to the shore again at **Otterbield Bay**.

Continue along the shore path, to join the main path again. Go through the gate ahead and continue along the shore—a lovely section of small bays and wooded headlands.

4. Pass the launch jetty at **Brandlehow** and, a little further on, skirt an area of old mining spoil. The right of way passes '**Brandlehow**' house, then bears left down the access track. At a fork, keep right and at the next cottage on the right, bear left, off the track, on a footpath that leads back down to the lake shore again at **Abbot's Bay**.

5. Follow the path ahead through the woods of **Manesty Park**. Immediately before the path leaves the woods, bear left to cross a stile on the edge of the water. Follow the path around the next wooded headland.

The path eventually joins the main footpath again where boardwalks

carry it over the boggy area where the **River Derwent** enters the lake.

Turn left, and follow the boardwalks

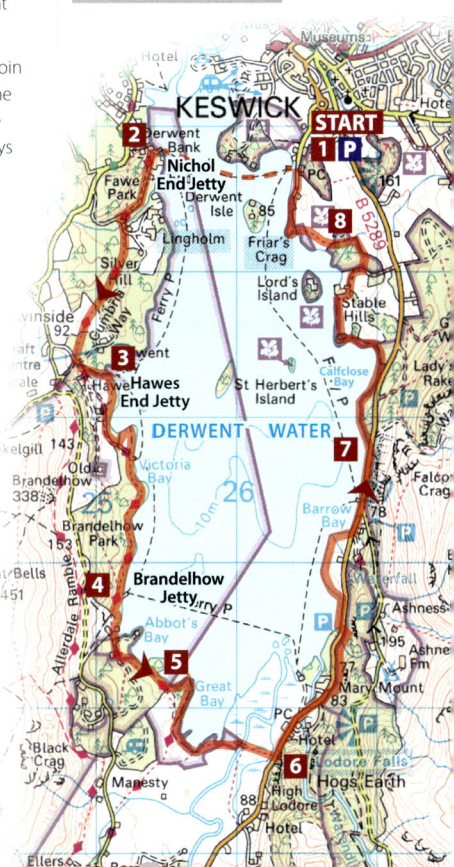

© Crown copyright and/or database right. All rights reserved. Licence number AC0000833184

Derwent Water's quiet wooded shores with Skiddaw rising behind

to cross the footbridge over the river. Continue ahead to reach the road.

6. Turn left and walk along the road past the **Lodore Falls Hotel**. There is a landing stage on the left just before the bridge.

Immediately before the **Mary Mount Hotel**, take the path on the right that runs parallel to the road.

At the **Kettlewell** car park, cross the road and take the shore path again. A permissive path heads round **Barrow Point**. Beyond the headland, the road runs tightly beside the lake. Although it is possible to continue along the shore, it becomes increasingly rocky. It's better to follow the road to the next wooded headland.

7. Drop down to the shore again and walk round into **Calfclose Bay**. Continue on the lakeside path, passing through the ancient yew trees on the next headland. Open fields follow, and as you approach cottages, keep to the right along the access drive. Within 250 metres, turn left through a gate and follow the path through **The Ings**, an area of wooded wetland.

8. The path emerges from the woods opposite wooded **Lord's Island**, then passes through National Trust land at **Strandshag Bay.** Pause here to enjoy the classic views across the lake to **Catbells**, set against the wooded foreground of **Friar's Crag**. Continue past Friar's Crag to eventually reach the road end. The road leads back to the landing stages to complete the walk. ♦

Derwent Isle

Derwent Isle is the only one of Derwent Water's four islands inhabited today. Hidden among the isle's trees is an intriguing 18th-century Italianate house owned by the National Trust but now leased as a private home. Its original owner, Henry Marshall, used to entertain the founders of the National Trust on the island, and today it's open to the public on just five days a year.

A peaceful morning at Loweswater

The autumn hues of Holme Wood are reflected in Loweswater

Continue on the lakeside footpath beyond the hut, crossing a footbridge over **Holme Beck**. At the far side of the woods the path swings left to rejoin the forest track. Turn right and go through the gate out of the woods.

7. Follow the track between open fields above the lake. At **Hudson Place**, go through the gate and turn right down the access road. In about 300 metres, take the signed footpath over the stile on the right. Follow the footpath ahead across the field. Boardwalks take you over marshy ground and a footbridge leads over the stream. Trace the footpath through the following fields to the lane, to complete the walk. ♦

Red squirrels

Beatrix Potter's Squirrel Nutkin made the red squirrel a Lake District icon. Today, the northern Lakes—and especially Holme Wood, at Loweswater—are among the best places in England to see our native red squirrels. Smaller and daintier than their American grey cousins, red squirrels have russet fur and tufted ears. Watch out for the squirrels' large nests or 'dreys' high in the trees.

A dramatic sunset at Castlerigg Stone Circle

The Walk

1. Opposite the layby is an access road signposted to 'Myre Syke' and 'Public Bridleway to **Mosser Fell Road**'. Follow the road as it rises steeply to a sharp lefthand bend. Ignore the road ahead to 'Myre Syke only'. Immediately after the bend, bear right onto a fenced path, which continues the climb to join the old fell road.

2. Turn sharp right along the fell road, now little more than a farm track. Follow the lane on its gentle descent back to **Loweswater**.

The easy walking will allow you to take in the wide views down to the lake with its beautiful woods backed by the fells of Carling Knott.

3. At the road turn left. In around 1.25km/¾ mile, turn right down the lane signed to 'Loweswater 0.8 miles'.

4. Follow the lane until it forks at the Loweswater National Trust sign. Bear right through a small car park, over the cattle grid, and continue along a farm access road towards the lake.

5. Just before **Watergate Farm**, bear right, off the track, across grass to rejoin the track by a gate that leads into **Holme Wood**. Go through the gate and follow the track ahead, which stays close to the lake shore on the right.

6. When you reach a small stone hut, bear right, off the forest track, and follow a narrower footpath that continues along the wooded shore.

The little shingle beach beside the hut is a good place to linger with its lovely views up the lake to the fells of Whiteside, Grasmoor, Whiteless Pike and Mellbreak.

LAKESIDE WALK

walk 6

Around **Loweswater**

An easy circuit of a small but pretty lake in a quiet corner of the Lake District

What to expect:
Woodland paths and quiet lanes. Mainly level walking with one steep ascent

Distance/time: 6.75 kilometres/ 4¼ miles. Allow 2 hours

Start: Layby at the western end of Loweswater lake on the minor lane linking the hamlet of Loweswater and Mockerkin

Grid ref: NY 118 224

Ordnance Survey Map: OL 4 *The English Lakes North-western area. Keswick, Cockermouth & Wigton*

After the walk: Kirkstile Inn, Loweswater

Walk outline
A steep climb on farm access roads leads to the old fell road high on the slopes of Low Fell with superb views of Loweswater and its surrounds. The fell road is followed back down through woods to the lane by the lake shore. Lanes, farm roads and forest tracks leads around the southern shore of the lake and on through Holme Wood. Good field paths are used to complete the route.

Loweswater
Hidden away in the top, northwest corner of the Lake District, sleepy Loweswater promises peace and quiet even in the height of summer. As the smallest of the lakes in the Buttermere valley, it also attracts fewer visitors than either Crummock Water or busy Buttermere.

Roughly a mile long by half a mile wide, and with a quiet road, cart tracks and paths around the shore, Loweswater provides the perfect, easy lakeside circuit for walkers. Along the way, look out for red squirrels and Holme Force waterfall in Holme Woods, or hire a traditional clinker built rowing boat from the National Trust at Watergate Farm.

Kirkstile Inn, Loweswater

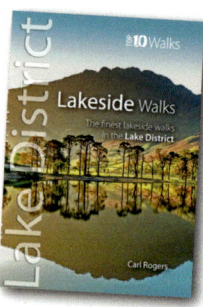

More lakeside walks ...

walk 7

A WALK WITH HISTORY

Castlerigg Stone Circle

A gentle ramble at the foot of the fells, starting and finishing at an enigmatic prehistoric site

What to expect:
Quiet lanes, low fell, tracks, farm paths, poor signposting

Distance/time: 6.5 kilometres/ 4 miles. Allow 2–2½ hours
Start: Roadside parking beside Castlerigg Stone Circle, about 1.5 kilometres east of Keswick
Grid ref: GR 291 237
Ordnance Survey Map: Explorer OL 4 The English Lakes *Northwestern area. Keswick, Cockermouth & Wigton*
After the walk: Horse and Farrier Inn, Thelkeld, near Keswick, Cumbria, CA12 4SQ. www.horseandfarrier.com | 017687 79688 | info@horseandfarrier.com

Walk outline

Setting off from the parking area beside Castlerigg Stone Circle—and always within sight of majestic Blencathra—the route uses quiet lanes and farm paths to reach Low Rigg. Passing lonely Tewet Tarn on the way, it climbs up and over this sometimes damp, low-lying fell to the church at St John's in the Vale. From here, a rough track heads downhill and then a series of farm paths are followed back to the stone circle.

Castlerigg Stone Circle

Castlerigg is one of the oldest stone circles in the country, dating back to about 3,000BC, the late Neolithic period. Nobody knows what the people of the New Stone Age would have used it for, although various theories have been put forward over the years. Was it an astronomical observatory? A religious site? Or maybe just a trading centre for hand axes? Today, its functions are many: from photographers' model and tourism attraction to a place of dawn pilgrimage every summer solstice.

Stone shadow

More walks with history …

The Walk

1. From the parking area, head east along the road for about 400 metres. You pass a group of buildings belonging to **Keswick Climbing Wall and Activity Centre** on your left. When you draw level with the white farmhouse in this group, turn right through a gate with a fingerpost beside it. Heading generally east, you now cross a series of fields via gates.

2. When you reach the next road, turn right. At the T-junction, turn right and, almost 300 metres later, right again along a quiet road—signposted 'St John's In The Vale church'.

3. About 350 metres along this road, turn right through a gate with a fingerpost beside it. A faint, grassy track winds its way up through the enclosure and then out through a gap in the top wall.

The way ahead isn't obvious. Head to the waist-high fingerpost about 80 metres to your right. Then, as indicated, bear left (south) to go through a stile about 30 metres up from the edge of **Tewet Tarn**. Head slightly right to pick up a grassy path beside the tarn.

Cross a stile next to a large gate. When the wall up to your right swings away, continue along the faint track (south)—crossing damp ground and then climbing slightly. After the next wall stile, keep straight ahead on the broad, grassy track. As you approach the buildings, the track appears to head off to the right. Ignore this; instead, cross the wall stile.

© Crown copyright and/or database right. All rights reserved. Licence number AC0000833184

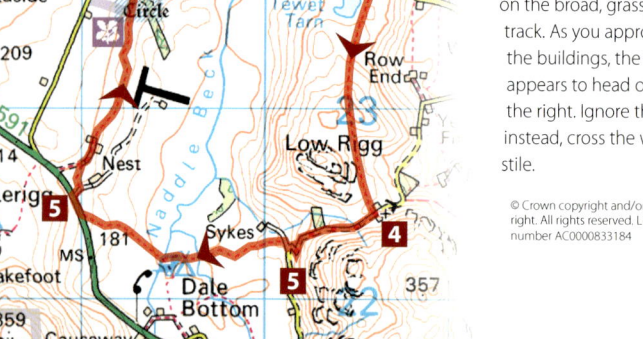

Walk 7 – **Castle Rigg Stone Circle** ♦ 43

The first rays of the rising sun catch Castlerigg's ancient standing stones

4. Turn right along the surfaced lane. This becomes a rough track that passes through a gate and then descends. When you reach an asphalt lane at the bottom of this drop, turn right and then immediately left through a kissing-gate just before the entrance to **Sykes Farm**.

5. The faint, grassy path heads to the right of the **rocky knoll** immediately in front of you and drops to another kissing-gate (west-south-west). Go through this and cross the next field in roughly the same direction to reach a gap between the fence and the wall in the field's far, right-hand corner. Go through the gap and make your way across damp ground to the **gated footbridge**. Cross this and continue west-south-west across the next field. Turn right on reaching a potentially soggy track—signposted A591. This ends just before reaching a gate.

Go through the gate and head gradually uphill with the fence/wall close by on your right. Cross an intervening wall via a stile about 40 metres in from the wall corner and then head straight across the next field to a gate in the top wall.

Castlerigg Stone Circle half silhouetted against low morning cloud

6. Turn right at the road and then right again along the track to **Low Nest Farm** —signposted 'Castlerigg Stone Circle'. Immediately after the cattle grid, go through the small gate on the left. Head uphill, following the line of the fence on your right. On reaching three gates, go through the middle one and turn right along the surfaced track.

Pass to the left of a **cottage** and then go through a large gate to the right of a converted barn. The path keeps close to the field boundary on your right and then goes through a small gate. Head straight across the next field (north-north-east) and go through a small gate in a drystone wall. Swing slightly left (north-north-west) to make for yet another small gate, beyond which you walk parallel with the wall up to your left. The faint path gradually eases its way up towards the fence on the left and then reaches the road. Turn left to return to **Castlerigg Stone Circle**.

If you haven't already visited it, go through one of the small gates on the left to enter the field in which the stone circle is located. An interpretation panel near one of the gates explains the circle's history and shows a model of the stones as they are today.

Just inside the eastern end of the circle is a group of 10 stones forming a rectangular enclosure known as 'The Sanctuary'. This mysterious feature is unique to Castlerigg. Excavations at the site have come up with few finds, although a stone axe head was unearthed in 1875. This is now in Keswick Museum. ♦

The second circle?

Castlerigg was first brought to the public's attention after it was visited by the antiquarian, Anglican clergyman and self-styled 'Druid' William Stukeley in 1725. His description of the stone circle forms the first written record of the site. It differs little from what can be seen today, although he claimed there was a second, even larger circle in a neighbouring field. However, no evidence has ever been found to back up this tantalising claim.

Looking towards the summit of Catbells from Skelgill Bank

A WALK ON THE LOW FELLS

walk 8

Catbells

Hawse End – Skelgill Bank – Catbells – Hause Gate – Allerdale Ramble – Hawse End

What to expect:
Good, clear fell paths along a grassy ridge with stunning views

Distance: 6.5 kilometres/ 4 miles
Ascent/descent: 380 metres/ 1,250 feet
Start: Limited free parking at Hawse End, near Gutherscale Lodge, on the minor road south of Portinscale and Swinside.
Grid ref: NY 247 213
Ordnance Survey Map: OL 4 *The English Lakes North-western area. Keswick, Cockermouth & Wigton*
Wainwrights: Catbells

Walk outline

The roadside parking at Hawse End soon gets congested on fine days. Yet within minutes you leave all that behind and head up the wonderful ridge of Skelgill Bank. It is everything a Lakeland ridge should be with narrow sections and some lovely rocky steps. A superb two kilometre walk brings you to the summit of Catbells. The scenic descent drops to the pass of Hause Gate. From here, a constructed path descends towards Derwent Water with the lake spread out below. Not far from the bottom an excellent track is joined to work an elevated route back to Hawse End.

Summit of Catbells

Catbells

Catbells is not quite as easy as some people think. The Skelgill Bank ridge is a stiff climb and the two main rocky steps—one in the lower reaches and another just below the summit—can be tricky and require care in bad weather.

Even so, the paths are good and the views spectacular, so save this walk for a clear day. Although the summit is often crowded, in the early morning or evening it is a wonderful place to soak up the surroundings, relax and daydream.

More walks on the low fells ...

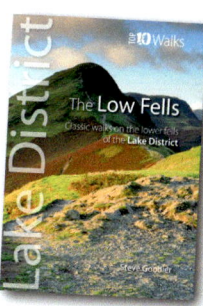

The Walk

1. From **Hawse End**, follow the road up to a cattle grid. Just before the grid, bear left through a gate and follow the path ahead, keeping the wire fence to your left. Continue uphill to the road and cross over, bearing half-left, to the broad path opposite.

A little farther on, leave the path, and cut back to the right, to take another steeply rising path. The path climbs steadily, kinks to the left, and continues upwards. Follow the path, which has steps in places, to the ridge end.

The path heads straight up for a while, before zig-zagging more steeply uphill. Occasional fences stop walkers from taking shortcuts and eroding the slopes. Higher up, continue past a path joining from the right that comes up from an alternative parking area below. Continue upwards to the end of **Skelgill Bank**.

2. Continue uphill along the ridge, which gradually becomes more defined. Climb up to a rock step below a memorial plaque. At the top, ascend easily at first and then more steeply along Skelgill Bank. Beyond a minor rocky top, the path continues along the ridge towards the summit of Catbells, now visible ahead.

The name Catbells probably comes from the Cumbrian dialect phrase 'Cat bields', meaning a place where 'wildcats shelter'. There is a place still called Cat Bields on Seatallen fell, near Wasdale.

© Crown copyright and/or database right. All rights reserved. Licence number AC0000833184

From Catbells the route continues to Hause Gate

Beyond a slight rise, the path drops down to a saddle where another path rises to join from the left. The path up the final slopes of Catbells is rough in parts. Although it forks occasionally, all routes eventually lead to the summit.

If you fancy more of a scramble to the top, bear left to the crest of the rising ridge, which leads to the base of another rock step. Scramble up and continue to the rocky **summit of Catbells**.

The 360° panorama from the broad, rocky summit is dominated by Derwent Water, far below. To the north are Keswick, Skiddaw, the Newlands Valley and Bassenthwaite Lake, while to the south is beautiful Borrowdale.

3. Drop south from the summit, descending carefully down a rocky step. Take the good path ahead, towards Maiden Moor. The path descends all the way to a fork just above the saddle of **Hause Gate**.

The old workings, spoil heaps and shafts close to Yewthwaite Gill, on the western side of the ridge below, are the remains of lead mines last worked in the 1890s.

Catbells enjoys panoramic views across Derwent Water to Keswick

4. Take the left-hand path here, which descends on a well-constructed route towards Derwent Water, below. The path snakes left and right to drop steeply down the fellside. Continue past an anti-erosion fence for a 100 metres or so, to reach a clear junction of paths.

5. Take the left-hand fork here, and head downhill again, now with the Manesty Park woods below to your right. Continue downhill to join a track alongside a wall on the right. Continue on the track, which rises past the wall.

Nearby is a bench and plaque commemorating the successful nineteenth-century novelist, Sir Hugh Walpole. Brackenburn Lodge, where he lived and worked from 1924 until 1941, overlooks Derwent Water below.

Continue to curve right between fences, with Derwent Water below to the right. The track is part of the long distance **Allerdale Ramble**. The path drops gently to the road below, to emerge at a marker post and a quarry parking area.

6. Take the path ahead that rises from the quarry, leaving the road behind. The path climbs for a while, then levels where another path joins from the left. The path climbs again before beginning a gradual descent in the direction of Skiddaw, ahead.

Walk on, to rejoin your outward route at the junction for the ridge climb. Descend to the road and cross it to a path opposite. Go through the gate by the cattle grid and return to the parking area to complete the walk. ♦

Fix the Fells

Around 10 million walkers use the Lake District's footpaths each year. Their pounding feet contribute to erosion that can be particularly bad on popular routes. Since 1993, the National Park Authority, National Trust and English Nature have been working together to manage the problem. Key techniques include 'soil inversion', and 'stone pitching': where naturally occurring rocks are dug into the ground to create firm footfalls.

Scafell Pike and Ill Crag from Eskdale

A WALK ON THE HIGH FELLS

walk 9

Scafell Pike

Seathwaite – Stockley Bridge – Esk Hause – Ill Crag – Broad Crag – Scafell Pike – Sty Head – Seathwaite

What to expect:
Well used, but rough fell paths over steep rocky terrain

Distance: 15.5 kilometres/ 9½ miles
Ascent/descent: 987 metres/ 3,240 feet
Start: Roadside parking at Seathwaite. Arrive early or expect to add a bit of road walking to the day's mileage
Grid ref: NY 235 123
Ordnance Survey Map: OL 4 *The English Lakes North-western area. Keswick, Cockermouth & Wigton*, OL 6 *The English Lakes South-western area. Coniston, Ulverston & Barrow-in-Furness*
Wainwrights: Ill Crag, Broad Crag, Scafell Pike

Walk outline

All paths to Scafell Pike pass through remote and wild terrain. From the lovely hamlet of Seathwaite, a good track climbs beyond Stockley Bridge and continues alongside Grains Gill and Ruddy Gill to reach Lakeland's highest pass, Esk Hause. The route continues up Calf Cove and then follows the broad, rugged ridge over Ill Crag and Broad Crag to reach the isolated summit of Scafell Pike. The traditional Corridor Route is used to descend to Sty Head and then onwards back to Seathwaite.

Scafell Pike

All Lakeland fell walkers turn their attention to Scafell Pike at some time: it is a beckoning beacon that cannot be ignored for long. And they are not disappointed, for Scafell Pike is a true mountain with rugged ascents and a magnificent summit that is exactly as the top of the highest ground in England should be.

Stockley Bridge

Despite the crowds, this is a great route and a superb area to explore. The subsidiary summits of Ill Crag and Broad Crag—both three thousand footers—are included, although Wainwright only gave them a minor section each in his books. Save this walk for a day of fine weather.

More walks on the high fells ...

Looking ahead to Scafell Pike from Broad Crag's rocky summit

The Walk

1. From **Seathwaite**, walk down the road to the farm and go through the **farmyard** following signs for 'Esk Hause and Sty Head Tarn'. Follow the farm track, and bear right where it forks.

The track continues above the infant **River Derwent**. Go through another gate, cross a side stream and continue along the track to **Stockley Bridge**.

2. Turn right across the bridge. Go through the gate here and turn immediately left, following the rising path through a gap in the fence.

The path climbs steadily alongside **Grains Gill**. Follow the path, cross a bridge over a side stream, and continue uphill, now with the tiny **Ruddy Gill** on your right. At the head of the gill, cross the stream on stepping stones. Bear left at a fork, climbing briefly again to a junction of paths.

3. Turn left here, rising steadily to bear right at a junction of paths. Continue up rock steps and over rough ground to a junction and cairn at **Esk Hause**.

4. Turn right here, shortly climbing a steep path up **Calf Cove**, which curves

Walk 9 – **Scafell Pike** ♦ 55

left to a large cairn, and climbs on up towards Ill Crag.

Follow the path as it levels slightly and then crosses a well-cairned boulder field. The summit of **Ill Crag** is over to the left; a visit is optional but should definitely be avoided in poor visibility.

5. From Ill Crag, the path drops to **Ill Crag col**. Climb the rough slopes towards Broad Crag on the far side. Cross another cairned boulder field, where the path passes below the summit of **Broad Crag**; again, an optional trip to the summit, up to the right, is not for misty days.

6. Beyond the boulder field, the path becomes distinct again. Descend roughly to cross **Broad Crag Col**. Scramble up the rocky rib ahead, following the path steeply up the slopes of **Scafell Pike**, using cairns to check the direction. Continue past a **wind shelter** to reach the summit.

7. With your back to the **summit cairn**, and facing the triangulation pillar, take the cairned path downhill, heading half-right, roughly northwards. The well-cairned path soon swings west, and descends towards **Lingmell Col**.

Watch for a **prominent cairn** on the right, immediately before the path swings left a little above Lingmell Col. This marks

© Crown copyright and/or database right. All rights reserved. Licence number AC0000833184

Great Gable, Green Gable and the Derwent Fells

the start of the **Corridor Route**, which descends over rough ground towards Sty Head Tarn, in the distance.

Keep ahead at a small junction, with a wall on the left, crossing a **beck**. Follow the path around the head of the rocky ravine of **Piers Gill**.

8. Beyond the gill, the path rises, curving around to the right. Pass a **small tarn** on the left, descending beneath the rocky summit of **Round How**, up to the right. The path rises, then drops to cross a **stream gully**.

Climb the exposed scramble carefully, continuing beyond to descend to, and eventually cross, a boggy area. The path rises to a cairned junction of paths, with a rocky knoll ahead. Go left here. Over a rise, the path crosses more boggy and stony ground then rises to **Sty Head Pass**, where there is a **Mountain Rescue stretcher** box at a junction of paths.

9. Turn right here, past a cairn, and descend past **Sty Head Tarn**. Continue ahead to cross the water flowing out of **Aaron Slack**, the gully on the left.

Soon afterwards, turn right over a bridge and then bear left, now on the righthand side of **Sty Head Gill**. Beyond a large cairn and a tributary stream, trace the edge of the gill downstream to reach a better path. Follow this downhill, eventually passing trees on the left. The path bends to the right, then descends back to **Stockley Bridge**.

Cross the bridge, turn left, and follow the track downhill back to **Seathwaite** to complete the walk. ♦

Wet, wet, wet!

Seathwaite is famous for being the wettest inhabited place in the country. The rain gauge that measures rainfall here is located near Sprinkling Tarn. The biggest downpour ever recorded during one 24-hour period in the UK was at Sprinkling Tarn in November 2009—a massive 314 millimetres, or more than one foot of rain. The deluge resulted in catastrophic flooding on the River Derwent in Keswick, Cockermouth and Workington.

Perfect conditions on Striding Edge

RIDGE WALK

walk 10

Striding & Swirral Edges

Patterdale – Lanty's Tarn – Hole-in-the-Wall – Striding Edge – Helvellyn – Swirral Edge – Catstycam – Glenridding

What to expect:
Spectacular rocky ridge scramble in ascent and descent. Good, well used fell paths

Distance: 12 kilometres/ sz7½ miles

Ascent/descent: 960 metres/ 3,150 feet

Start: The National Park car park in the centre of Glenridding.

Grid ref: NY 385 169

Ordnance Survey Map: OL 5 The English Lakes North-eastern area. *Penrith, Patterdale & Caldbeck*

Wainwright summits: Helvellyn, Catstycam

Walk outline

Easy walking to Lanty's Tarn to gain the Grisedale path followed by a long moderate ascent to the ridge crest. Straightforward low-grade scrambling on a narrow rock ridge with some exposure to reach Helvellyn's high summit plateau. A shorter scrambling descent via Swirral Edge, then easier walking to the shapely summit of Catstycam. The long easy-angled Glenridding path provides a return route.

Striding Edge & Swirral Edge

The most famous and popular mountains and hills in any area are usually the highest—Snowdon in North Wales, Ben Nevis in Scotland—but in the Lake District Helvellyn seems to have jumped the queue and knocked Scafell Pike off the number one spot. One reason for this is undoubtedly the inaccessibility of the latter. Helvellyn, on the other hand, rises directly from a main road which runs through the heart of the district. It is also one of the four highest summits in the Lake District and it has perhaps the most famous ridge walk in the country—Striding Edge. This narrow airy arête is justifiably famous and provides one of the best mountain experiences to be had on the Lakeland fells.

Swirral Edge in winter

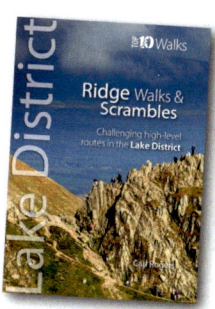

More ridge walks ...

Walkers following the narrow crest of Striding Edge

The Walk

1. Leave the car park by the lower entrance and turn right along the road to cross the **bridge**. Turn right immediately (opposite the '**Glenridding Hotel**') and walk along the lane between the river and the shops.

At the end of the access lane by **stone house**s, go left over the **footbridge** and follow the pitched footpath up through **woods**. Leaving the woods the path veers right across the open hillside.

2. At a gate in the **wall ahead,** don't go through; instead turn sharp left and follow the path up to **Lanty's Tarn**, in its small hollow and surrounded by pines.

Follow the path past the tarn, then bear right off the main path on a narrower footpath that heads across grass to enter and pass through a **small wood** by gates. Beyond the wood the path descends to join the main path coming up from **Grisedale**.

Grisedale is a beautiful valley and there are superb views from here up to the head of the dale to the shapely summits of Nethermost Pike, Dollywaggon Pike and St Sunday Crag.

Turn right and follow the broad path climbing steadily up towards the famous '**Hole-in-the-Wall**'—a gap in the wall that can be seen running up the hillside to the skyline ahead. The path is never steep, but it is much further than it looks to the skyline (over 2 kilometres/1½ miles).

As you gain height there are increasing views left into Grisedale and up to the head of the valley.

The ridge crest is a good place for a break. Here the impressive east face of Helvellyn, with the enclosing arms of Striding Edge and Swirral Edge, can be seen for the first time rising above Red Tarn which occupies the bottom of the combe (out of sight until you are further along the ridge).

3. Cross the stile here ('Hole in the Wall') and continue on the path ahead. **Striding Edge** starts with the small **summit of Low Spying How**, a good place to take stock of the ridge ahead.

The first section is composed of clean blocky rock with very little grass, the second half is narrower with a sharper

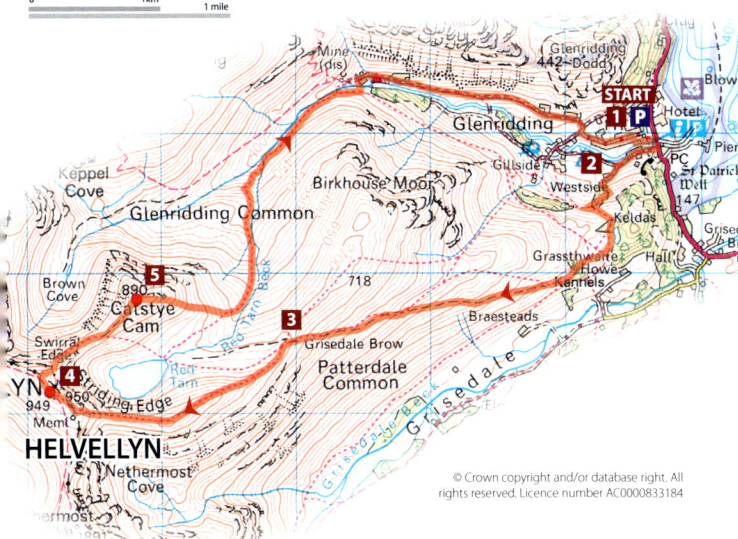

© Crown copyright and/or database right. All rights reserved. Licence number AC0000833184

Scramblers on the crest of Striding Edge with views to St Sunday Crag and Fairfield

crest but more broken rocks. **NB—Nowhere is the scrambling 'difficult' but it is fairly exposed, so you will need good balance and a head for heights. The less adventurous can avoid the crest by a traversing path a little way down on the right.**

The final obstacle on the ridge provides the crux—a **squat rock tower** requiring a short scramble descent to a narrow gap at the point where the ridge merges into the broken upper slopes of the mountain. Easier scrambling, then steep scree lead onto the summit plateau where you will enjoy the fine classic view back along the ridge.

Head right along the plateau rim past the cross-shaped **stone wind shelter** to **Helvellyn summit** marked by a **triangulation pillar**.

Helvellyn is one of the few Lakeland summits where almost every other fell is visible. The most striking panorama is westwards, where you should be able to see the Coniston Fells, Bowfell, Crinkle Crags, Esk Pike and Scafell Pike. Great Gable is probably the most prominent and striking of all. The Derwent Fells and Skiddaw complete the view to the northwest.

4. Beyond the summit a small **cairn** marks the exit point from the plateau

Walk 10 – **Striding & Swirral Edges** ♦ 63

onto **Swirral Edge**. This is both easier and shorter than Striding Edge, but still requires care. The broken rocks soon merge into grass as the angle eases on the broad saddle between Helvellyn and Catstycam.

A good path bears right from here to the outflow of **Red Tarn** where it joins the Glenridding path, but Catstycam is too good a summit to leave out and is easily gained by the gentle ridge ahead.

The view back to Helvellyn rising above Red Tarn from here is superb, particularly under winter conditions, or when late snow lingers on this sheltered northeast face.

5. From the **summit of Catstycam**, descend the rounded east ridge on the path that sweeps down to join the Glenridding path beside **Red Tarn Beck**.

Follow this path down beside the beck into the lower valley. The path then stays close to the broader **Glenridding Beck**. Cross the beck by the large **wooden footbridge** on the left and follow the path right, soon passing **Glenridding Youth Hostel** to join the unsurfaced lane which can be followed easily back to **Glenridding** to complete the route (about 2 kilometres/1½ miles). ♦

Useful Information

Cumbria Tourism
Cumbria Tourism's official website covers everything from accommodation and events to attractions and adventure. **www.golakes.co.uk**

Lake District National Park
The Lake District National Park website also has information on things to see and do, plus maps, webcams and news. **www.lakedistrict.gov.uk**

Tourist Information Centres
The main TICs provide free information on everything from accommodation and travel to what's on and walking advice.

Ambleside	01539 432 582	amblesidetic@southlakeland.gov.uk
Grasmere	01539 435 245	grasmeretic@lake-district.gov.uk
Bowness	01539 442 895	bownesstic@lake-district.gov.uk
Coniston	01539 441 533	mail@conistontic.org
Keswick	01768 772 645	keswicktic@lake-district.gov.uk
Penrith	01768 867 466	pen.tic@eden.gov.uk
Ullswater	01768 482 414	ullswatertic@lake-district.gov.uk
Windermere	01539 446 499	info@windermereinfo.co.uk

Steamers and Ferries
Four lakes have regular, year round 'steamers', launches or ferries.

Windermere	01539 443 360	www.windermere-lakecruises.co.uk info@windermere-lakecruises.co.uk
Derwentwater	01768 772 263	www.keswick-launch.co.uk info@keswick-launch.co.uk
Coniston	01539 432 733	www.nationaltrust.org.uk/steam-yacht-gondola sygondola@nationaltrust.org.uk
	01768 775 753	www.conistonlaunch.co.uk info@conferry.co.uk
Ullswater	01768 482 229	www.ullswater-steamers.co.uk enquiries@ullswater-steamers.co.uk

Weather
Five day forecast for the Lake District: 0844 846 2444
www.lakedistrict.gov.uk/weatherline